The Book of
the Bible
made easy

Mark Water

HENDRICKSON PUBLISHERS

The Books of the Bible Made Easy
Hendrickson Publishers, Inc.
P.O. Box 3473
Peabody, Massachusetts 01961-3473

First printing — May 2001

Manufactured in China

Contents

Special pull-out chart
Linking up Bible books

Genesis
The book of beginnings

"In the beginning God created the heavens and the earth."
Genesis 1:1

Major theme
Beginnings of creation, Satan, sin, nations, peoples and God's plan to reclaim all of humanity.

Background and purpose
Genesis is the history of origins, including the creation of the world, the entrance of sin and death, and the rise of nations. It records the fall of human beings and the first prophecy of Christ's defeat of Satan and the reclaiming of humanity *(3:15)*.

Author
The book's author is not named, however, both Jews and Christians have attributed the first five books of the Bible to Moses.

Date
The exact date of writing is not known. Possibly Moses wrote it while in the wilderness, during the 40-year period in which God's children wandered aimlessly in the desert, when God met with Moses on Mount Sinai. The best guess is approximately 1400 BC.

Brief outline

1. Creation and the fall *1:1–5:32*

2. Noah and his descendants *6:1–11:26*

3. Abram (Abraham and his descendants) *11:27–25:18*

4. Issac *25:19–26:43*

5. Jacob and Esau *27:1–36:43*

6. The story of Joseph *37:1–50:26*

Important events
- **Creation** God is the Creator
- **Fall** Adam sins against God
- **Flood** God's judgment
- **Nations** After the building of the Tower of Babel God scatters people over the face of the earth.
- **Israel** The foundation of God's chosen people.

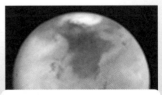

Christ in Genesis
- **Christ** is seen as a "type" in Genesis. He is depicted in various events and people.
- A "type" is an historical fact which illustrates a spiritual truth. For example: Adam is the head of the human race. Christ is the Head of the new creation.

Exodus
The book of departure

"Therefore, say to the Israelites: 'I am the Lord, and I will bring you out from under the yoke of the Egyptians. I will free you from being slaves to them, and I will redeem you with an outstretched arm and with mighty acts of judgment.'" *Exodus 6:6*

Major theme
Exodus records the slavery, deliverance and beginnings of the people of Israel on their journey to Canaan.

Background and purpose
Exodus describes God's actions as he liberated his enslaved people and molded them into a nation. Moses is the central figure. God chose him to miraculously lead the people of Israel out of Egypt, triumphing through the Red Sea into Sinai. God gives Moses the ten commandments on Mount Sinai. He directs the Israelites to make a chest, the ark of testimony (ark of the covenant), which is to be housed in the tabernacle.

Author
The book's author is not named, however, both Jews and Christians have attributed the first five books of the Bible to Moses.

Date
Approximately 1400 BC. The exact date of writing is not known. Possibly Moses kept an account of God's work which he then wrote out in the plains of Moab before he died.

Brief outline
1. The Israelites delivered from Egypt *1:1–15:21*
2. Traveling from the Red Sea to Mount Sinai *15:22–18:27*
3. Giving the Law and the covenant *19:1–24:18*
4. The tabernacle and instructions for worship *25:1–40:38*

5

Important events
- The Israelites are made slaves
- The ten plagues
- The Passover
- The escape from Egypt
- The giving of the ten commandments

Christ in Exodus
- The Passover lamb *(12:3)*, is a type of Christ, who is the Lamb of God
- Manna *(16:4)*, is a type of Christ.

Leviticus
The book of atonement

"'I am the Lord your God;
consecrate yourselves and be holy,
because I am holy.'"
Leviticus 11:44

Major theme
Leviticus carries on from the
end of Exodus without a break,
describing the God-given
sacrificial rituals and practices
for worship. Holiness and the
perfection of God is portrayed
throughout the book.

Background and purpose
The book answers the
question: How can sinful
humans approach a holy God?
The words "holy" and
"holiness" occur over 150
times. Leviticus is filled with
laws defining the ways in
which God's people are to
worship. The people are
instructed to keep their
relationship with God alive,
and to live holy lives.

Author
The author is not named.
Throughout the book is the
continuing statement, "The
Lord spoke to Moses."

Date
Approximately 1400 BC. Much
of the material recorded was
given to Moses by God at
Mount Sinai.

Brief outline

1. Regulations for sacrifices and
   offerings *1:1–7:38*

2. The priesthood and the
   tabernacle *8:1–10:20*

3. Cleanness and uncleanness
   11:1–15:33

4. The day of atonement *16:1–34*

5. Regulations about living
   17:1–22:33

6. Instructions for national life
   23:1–27:34

Important events

Regulations about sacrifices

The five annual feasts

1. The Feast of the Passover

2. The Feast of Pentecost

3. The Feast of Trumpets

4. The Day of Atonement

5. The Feast of Tabernacles

Christ in Leviticus
• Jesus is our great high priest.
• The scapegoat *(16:20-22)*, bore
  the sins of Israel, as Jesus bears
  our sins.

Numbers
Wandering in the desert

"'... not one of the men who saw my glory and the miraculous signs I performed in Egypt and in the desert but who disobeyed me and tested me ten times–not one of them will ever see the land I promised on oath to their forefathers.'" *Numbers 14:22-23*

Major theme
Two themes are apparent: God is faithful to his people, but disobedience is always punished.

Background and purpose
While Leviticus covers only a short period of time, Numbers covers nearly 39 years. It records Israel's movements from the last days at Mount Sinai, the wanderings around Kadesh-barnea, to the arrival in the plains of Moab in the fortieth year. This resulted from Israel's disbelief and disobedience to God. For Israel, what could have been an eleven-day journey became forty years of wandering in the desert.

This book is given the name "Numbers" in the *Septuagint*, the pre-Christian Greek translation of the Old Testament. This name is derived from the two occasions on which the Israelites were numbered, *chapters 1 and 39*.

Author
The book's author is not named. Traditionally, both Jews and Christians have attributed the first five books of the Bible to Moses.

Date
Approximately 1400 BC.

Brief outline

1. Israelites prepare to leave Mount Sinai *1:1–4:49*

2. More laws of God for the people *5:1–10:10*

3. Wandering in the wilderness, from Mount Sinai to Moab *10:11–21:35*

4. Events in Moab and summary of the journey from Egypt to Moab *22:1–33:49*

5. Instructions before crossing the Jordan *33:50–36:13*

Christ in Numbers
- The offering of the red heifer *(chapter 19)*, symbolizes salvation through Jesus' offering of himself.
- Jesus himself pointed to the bronze serpent *(21:1-9)*, and said, "So the Son of Man must be lifted up" *(John 3:14)*.

Deuteronomy
God's laws

"Love the Lord your God with all your heart and with all your soul and with all your strength."
Deuteronomy 6:5

Major theme
God renews his covenant with Israel on the plains of Moab just before they enter the Promised Land.

Background and purpose
The term deuteronomy signifies the "Second law." The original teaching of Moses (from God) is repeated, commented upon, explained and enlarged because those who first heard the teachings were now dead, except for Moses, Joshua, and Caleb. This book records three of Moses' speeches and his last words. Through this teaching Moses confirms Israel as God's people before handing over his leadership of them to Joshua. He tells them to remember God when they prosper and that they will be disciplined if they disobey God.

Author
The book's author is not named. However, both Jews and Christians have attributed the first five books of the Bible to Moses. It has been pointed out that Moses could hardly be the author of a book which records his own last words. But Moses could still be the author of everything except the introduction *(1:1-5)*, and the report of his death *(34)*. Jesus spoke about Moses being the author of this book *(Matthew 19:7-8; Mark 10:3-5; John 5:46-47)*.

Date
Approximately 1400 BC.

Brief outline

1. Review of the Israelites journey from Eygpt *1:1–4:43*

2. The ten commandments and loving God *4:44–6:25*

3. Moses' teachings from God reviewed *7:1–26:19*

4. Moses reviews Israel's pledged relationship with God *27:1–30:20*

5. Moses and his final days *31:1–34:12*

Christ in Deuteronomy
- Moses, probably more than any other Old Testament person, is a "type" of Jesus.
- Jesus quoted Scripture more often from the book of Deuteronomy than from any other Old Testament book.

8

Joshua
Conquering the Promised Land

"'Have I not commanded you? Be strong and courageous. Do not be terrified; do not be discouraged, for the Lord your God will be with you wherever you go.'" *Joshua 1:9*

Major theme

The account of how God kept his promise to bring his people into the Promised Land. The book's theme is "... take possession of the land the Lord your God is giving you for your own" *(1:11)*.

Background and purpose

The book of Joshua was written to document the initial fulfilment of God's promises to Abraham, Issaac, and Jacob, as the people of God enter Canaan. It records the Israelite invasion of the Promised Land, the partitioning of the Promised Land and the settling down in the Promised Land. Joshua is full of military battles, specific towns, and places. The spiritual principles used in Joshua are the same principles to be used in the spiritual battles faced by all generations of God's followers. *See Hebrews 4:1-11*

Author

According to Jewish tradition and Joshua 24:26 the author was Joshua: "And Joshua recorded these things in the Book of the Law of God."

Date

Approximately 1350 BC. Joshua was probably written in the early days of the Judges of Israel.

Brief outline

1. Entering the land
   1:1–5:12

2. Conquering the land
   5:13–12:15

3. Distributing the land
   13:1–21:45

4. Joshua's farewell
   22:1-24:33

9

Christ in Joshua

- "The commander of the army of the Lord" *(5:14)*, was an appearance of Jesus.

Judges
Israel's twelve judges

"In those days Israel had no king; everyone did as he saw fit."
Judges 21:25
["… did what was right in his own eyes." New King James Version]

Major theme
The book of Judges is the link between Joshua bringing the Israelites into the Promised Land and Saul, David and the other kings of Israel. Through the book the Israelites fall into chaos and desert God – yet there is a loving God who disciplines them, loves them and refuses to give up on them.

Background and purpose
The twelve "judges" in this book were not only concerned with legal matters but were charismatic military leaders. The book is made up of six periods of oppression covering approximately 300 years. The following "sin-cycle" is repeated:
• A time of peace. God is ignored. Pagan gods replace God.
• A time of oppression. Israel is attacked.
• A time of repentance. Israel turns back to God.
• A time of deliverance. God sends a judge and delivers Israel.
• A time of peace. God is ignored again and the "sin-cycle" starts once more.
The apostasy illustrated in Judges shows why the people

felt they needed a king and leads on to the books of Samuel and Kings.

Author
The book's author is not named. Samuel or one of his prophetic students may have written it. Another suggestion is that a prophet such as Nathan or Gad, who were linked to David's court, may have written it.

Date
Various dates have been suggested and an eleventh century or tenth century BC date is probable.

Brief outline

1. Conquest of Canaan retold
  1:1–3:6

2. Israel under the judges' oppression and deliverance
  3:7–16:31

3. The religious and moral failings under the judges *17:1–21:25*

Christ in Judges
• Jesus is seen as our Deliverer.

Ruth
Human loyalty

"But Ruth replied, 'Don't urge me to leave you or to turn back from you. Where you go I will go, and where you stay I will stay. Your people will be my people and your God my God.'"
Ruth 1:16

Major theme
Ruth, a Moabite widow, because of the love for her mother-in-law, Naomi, leaves her own country and travels back with Naomi to Bethlehem. There she meets Boaz, a relative of Naomi, who marries her.

Background and purpose
The book of Ruth singles out one family that lived in the time of the judges *(1:1)*. The book illustrates that the blesssings of God came to non-Jews as well as Jews. The genealogy at the end of the book shows that Ruth, a non-Jewish woman, became the grandmother of King David and an ancestor of Jesus. *See Matthew 1:5*

Author
The author is unknown. Samuel was the author according to a Talmudic tradition. But this is unlikely since David is mentioned *(4:17,22)*, and Samuel died before David's coronation *(1 Samuel 25:1)*.

Date
It seems likely that Ruth was written in the time of the kings of Israel and so an eleventh century or tenth century BC date is probable.

Brief outline

1. Ruth and Naomi return to Bethlehem *1:1-22*

2. Ruth meets Boaz *2:1–3:18*

3. Boaz marries Ruth *4:1-22*

11

Christ in Ruth
• Jesus is our Kinsman-redeemer.

1 & 2 Samuel
Israel's first kings

"'Does the Lord delight in burnt
  offerings and sacrifices
as much as in obeying the voice
  of the Lord?
To obey is better than sacrifice,
  and to heed is better than the
  fat of rams.'"
1 Samuel 15:22

"And David knew that the Lord
had established him as king over
Israel and had exalted his
kingdom for the sake of his people
Israel." *2 Samuel 5:12*

Major theme
1 and 2 Samuel are a single
book in the Hebrew Bible.
1 Samuel continues the history
of Israel from the time of the
judges to the founding of the
monarchy under Saul.
2 Samuel records David's
successes and failures as king.

Background and purpose
1 Samuel records the birth,
childhood and ministry of
Samuel, the life of Saul and
the first part of David's life.

2 Samuel records David as
king at Hebron and then at
Jerusalem and David's last
days. Jerusalem becomes the
religious capital of Israel.

Author
The author's name is not
stated. The Talmudic tradition
states that Samuel was the
author, but since his death is
recorded in 1 Samuel 25:1 he
couldn't have written the
whole book.

Date
The anonymous author must
have lived after Solomon's
death in 930 BC, and after the
division of the kingdom since
"Israel and Judah" are
mentioned in 1 Samuel 11:8
and 2 Samuel 5:5. This means
that the writing took place
sometime between 930 BC and
722 BC

Brief outline

1 Samuel

1. Samuel judges Israel *1:1–8:22*

2. Saul as first King of Israel
  9:1–15:35

3. Saul and David *16:1–31:13*

2 Samuel

1. David reigns over Judah
  1:1–6:23

2. David expands the kingdom
  7:1–10:19

3. David's sins and their
  consequences *11:1–20:26*

4. The conclusion of the kingdom
  under David *21:1–24:25*

Christ in 1 & 2 Samuel
- **1 Samuel** Samuel is a type of
  Jesus.
- **2 Samuel** David is one of the
  main Old Testament portrayals
  of Jesus.

1 & 2 Kings
The kingdom is united and then divided

"So the Lord said to Solomon, 'Since this is your attitude and you have not kept my covenant and my decrees, which I commanded you, I will most certainly tear the kingdom away from you and give it to one of your subordinates.'" *1 Kings 11:11*

"So the people of Israel were taken from their homeland into exile in Assyria ..." *2 Kings 17:23*

Major theme
1 and 2 Kings was originally a single book, tracing the history of God's people from the death of David to their deportation to Babylon.

Background and purpose
In 1 Kings Israel is united, Solomon builds the temple and then the kingdom of Israel is divided.

2 Kings records the ministry of Elijah and Elisha and the capture of Israel and Judah.

The books depict the consequences of obedience and disobedience to God. The story of the two nations of Israel and Judah is presented in a systematic form. An account of the events in the life of a king of Israel is followed by an account of the events in the lives of all the kings of Judah who reigned at the same time. 1 Kings shows an illustrious beginning for the kingdom of Israel. 2 Kings shows the affect of a broken kingdom as seen in the spiritual hollowness in the lives of the people.

Author
The author is not known. Talmudic tradition refers to the prophet Jeremiah.

Date
It is possible for a single author living in exile to have used the source materials available to him and to have written 1 and 2 Kings around 560 BC.

Brief outline

1 Kings

1. David's death *1:1–2:11*

2. Solomon's reign *2:12–11:43*

3. Israel divided: Northern and Southern kingdoms *12:1–22:53*

2 Kings

1. The divided kingdom to Israel's fall *1:1–17:41*

2. Kings in the surviving nation of Judah *18:1–21:26*

Christ 1 & 2 Kings
- **1 Kings** Solomon is a "type" of Jesus. Jesus himself said, "'... one greater than Solomon is here'" *(Matthew 12:42)*.
- **2 Kings** Elisha is a "type" of Jesus, while Elijah is a "type" of John the Baptist.

1 & 2 Chronicles
David's reign and Israel's apostasy

"'I will set him [David] over my house and my kingdom for ever; his throne will be established for ever.'" *1 Chronicles 17:14*

"'... if my people, who are called by my name, will humble themselves and pray and seek my face and turn from their wicked ways, then will I hear from heaven and will forgive their sin and will heal their land.'" *2 Chronicles 7:14*

Major theme

1 and 2 Chronicles covers the same period of the history of God's people as that described in 2 Samuel through 2 Kings. Chronicles views these events from a spiritual perspective, whereas 2 Samuel and 1 and 2 Kings traces them from more of a political standpoint.

Background and purpose

1 and 2 Chronicles emphasize that God is still with his people. Although God's people were living in a secular environment and their nation had been nearly destroyed by war, God had brought them back to Jerusalem. 1 and 2 Chronicles explain why the history of God's people took the course it did and why it is still possible to have faith. God's people are told to learn from the mistakes of history.

Author

1 and 2 Chronicles is one book in the Hebrew Bible.
The author is not known, but according to an old Jewish tradition Ezra wrote the book.
1 and 2 Chronicles is a compilation drawn from many written sources.

Date

It is quite possible that the book was written, if not by Ezra himself, in Ezra's lifetime, in the last half of the fifth century BC.

Brief outline

1 Chronicles

1. Genealogies from Adam to Saul *1:1–9:44*

2. The death of Saul *10:1-14*

3. David's reign *11:1–29:30*

2 Chronicles

1. Solomon's reign *1:1–9:31*

2. The history of Judah *10:1–36:12*

3. The fall of Jerusalem *36:13-23*

Christ in 1 & 2 Chronicles

- **Jesus** is King of kings and Lord of lords.

14

Ezra
Return from Babylon

This is what Cyrus King of Persia says: "'may his God be with him, and let him go up to Jerusalem in Judah and build the temple of the Lord, the God of Israel, the God who is in Jerusalem.'" *Ezra 1:3*

Major theme
Restoration: The return of the exiles from Babylon to Jerusalem.

Background and purpose
Ezra is a sequel to 1 and 2 Chronicles. It helps us to understand the background for the prophecies of Malachi. Chapters 1–6 show the providence of God as they describe how Cyrus' decree allows the exiles to return to Jerusalem under Zerubbabel, and the rebuilding of the temple. Chapters 7–10 describe the return under Ezra along with his moral and religious reforms which help to safeguard the spiritual heritage of Israel.

Author
The author is not named, but the Talmud attributes the book to Ezra. Some of the book is written in the first person from Ezra's point of view.

Date
The middle of the fifth century BC, approximately 440 BC.

Brief outline

1. Cyrus' decree to return to Jerusalem *1:1-11*

2. The first group of exiles return to Jerusalem *2:1-70*

3. The rebuilding of the temple *3:1–6:22*

4. Ezra returns to Jerusalem *7:1–10:44*

Christ in the book of Ezra
- **Jesus** is the Lord of heaven and earth.
- The book of Ezra typifies Jesus' work of restoration and forgiveness.

Nehemiah
Rebuilding Jerusalem's walls

"But we prayed to our God and posted a guard day and night to meet this threat." *Nehemiah 4:10*

Major theme
Chapters 1–7 describe Nehemiah's restoration of the walls of Jerusalem. Chapters 8–13 record Ezra's and Nehemiah's reforms. Nehemiah fully trusted in God as he prayed and planned for the rebuilding of the walls. Even facing opposition, his faith did not waver.

Background and purpose
The book of Nehemiah, which serves as a natural sequel to the book of Ezra, shows how God's providential hand re-established his people in their homeland after their exile. Without walls Jerusalem could not be thought of as a city at all. So Nehemiah's first priority was to rebuild the walls of Jerusalem. Nehemiah constantly reveals his dependence on God in his frequent prayers. The book of Nehemiah fills in the background to the three prophetic books of Haggai, Zechariah and Malachi.

Author
The book opens with the words, "The words of Nehemiah son of Hacaliah"

(1:1). The book of Nehemiah is the only Old Testament first-person narrative written by an important Jewish leader.

Date
The fifth century BC, approximately 430 BC, some time after the 32nd year of Artaterxes, king of Persia.

Brief outline

1. Nehemiah returns to Jerusalem *1:1–2:20*

2. Jerusalem's walls are rebuilt *3:1–7:73*

3. The Law is read and the covenant renewed *8:1–10:39*

4. Jerusalem is organized and revival spreads *11:1–13:31*

Christ in Nehemiah
- Nehemiah portrays Jesus in Jesus' work of restoration.

Esther
God rules behind the scenes

"'For if you remain silent at this time, relief and deliverance for the Jews will arise from another place, but you and your father's family will perish. And who knows but that you have come to royal position for such a time as this?'"
Esther 4:14

Major theme
Esther becomes queen to the Persian King, Xerxes. Driven by his hatred for Mordecai, Haman plots to exterminate the Jews. Esther cleverly persuades the king to reverse his decision against the Jews and Haman is hanged.

Background and purpose
The book of Esther explains the origin of the Feast of Purim, which the Jews celebrate between 13th and 15th Adar (February-March). *See 3:7; 9:20-32.* The book of Esther does not mention the name of God, although the name of a pagan king is mentioned over 150 times. God's power is apparent and is seen in his divine control and intervention.

Author
The author is not named. The contents of the book reveal that the author was Jewish and had first hand knowledge about Persian etiquette and customs. Esther or a younger contemporary of Mordecai have been suggested as possible authors.

Date
The book is set in the reign of Ahasuerus, the Hebrew name, or Xerxes, the Greek name, of Khshayarsh, king of Persia in 486–464 BC. The book of Esther was probably written in the middle of the fifth century BC.

Brief outline
1. Esther becomes queen of Persia *1:1–2:23*
2. Haman's plot and Esther's intervention *3:1–5:14*
3. Haman is executed *6:1–7:10*
4. The Jews defend themselves; the Feast of Purim *8:1–10:3*

17

Christ in Esther
- Esther, like Jesus, put herself in the place of death for her people when she seeks the king's approval. Esther portrays Jesus' work as Advocate on our behalf.

Job
Why do the innocent suffer?

"'But he knows the way I take;
when he has tested me, I shall
come forth as gold.'"
Job 23:10

Major theme
Job was a "blameless and
upright" man (*1:1*) who lost
everything, which seems totally
unjust. In three cycles of
debate with his friends, they
argue that God judges the
wicked and conclude that Job
must be wicked. Job challenges
the reader with the difficult
question, "If God is a God of
mercy, why do the righteous
suffer?"

Background and purpose
The book of Job does not
explain the reason for innocent
suffering but rather gives Job a
glimpse of God's greatness,
goodness and wisdom. *See
38:1–42:6.* In chapter 42 Job
acknowledges God's majesty
and sovereignty and stops
demanding an answer to the
"why?" of his situation.

Author
The author is not named.
Although most of the book is
made up of the words of Job
and his "counselors", Job was
probably not the author of the
book. The unknown author of
the book must have been a
Jew, for he (but not Job and his
friends) use Yahweh (NIV
"the Lord") as the name for
God. Some have credited
Moses or Solomon as the
author.

Date
No one knows for certain
when the book was written.
Some claim that it is the oldest
book in the Bible with a date of
2000–1800 BC It is clearly
possible that it could have
been written at any time from
King Solomon's reign to the
exile. A date as early as the
tenth century BC is sometimes
favored.

Brief outline
1. Prologue: Job's test *1:1–2:13*
2. The false comfort of Job's
   friends *3:1–31:40*
3. Elihu's advice *32:1–37:24*
4. God's speaks to Job *38:1–42:6*
5. Epilogue: Job's restoration
   42:7-17

Christ in Job
• Job acknowledges a Redeemer,
  (19:25-27), and calls out for a
  Mediator *(9:33; 25:4; 33:23)*.

18

Psalms
The book of devotion and praise

"Come, let us sing for joy to the Lord; let us shout aloud to the Rock of our salvation."
Psalms 95:1

Major theme
The psalms reveal a loving God who is not only the Savior and Shepherd of his own people, but also the Creator, Sustainer, Judge and King of the whole world.

Background and purpose
The name of the book of Psalms comes from a Greek word meaning "a song sung to the accompaniment of a plucked instrument." The psalms were the hymn-book of the Israelites. They were used in the two temples as well as for personal use. A large number of themes are included in the psalms but their common theme is worship. The intent of the psalms is to kindle in the souls of men and women a devotion and affection for God, the Creator and Lord.

Author
Most people automatically think of David as being the author of the psalms. From the superscriptions at the head of all but 34 of the psalms, it is possible to conclude David wrote 73 of the psalms, the sons of Korah wrote ten of them, Asaph wrote twelve of them, Solomon wrote two of them, "Moses the man of prayer" wrote one *(Psalm 90)*, and Heman and Ethan also wrote one each. The book of Psalms is "a collection of collections," as the 150 psalms are split up into five "books."

Date
The psalms cover a wide period of time. Scholars date some of them back as far as Moses, with some written in the times of Ezra and Nehemiah. Most of the psalms were written in the tenth century BC.

Brief outline

1. Book *1*	1–41
2. Book *2*	42–72
3. Book *3*	73–89
4. Book *4*	90–106
5. Book *5*	107–150

Christ in Psalms
Many psalms have direct or typical references to Jesus:
• Jesus as King *(2; 45; 72; 110)*
• Jesus' sufferings *(22; 41)*
• Jesus' resurrection *(16)*
• Jesus' ascension *(68:18)*

Proverbs
Maxims to live by

"Trust in the Lord with all your
heart
and lean not on your own
understanding;
in all your ways acknowledge him,
and he will make your paths
straight."
Proverbs 3:5-7

Major theme
The key theme in Proverbs is
wisdom, which is mentioned
one hundred and four times.
Proverbs points out that this
wisdom is available to
everyone. Wise people are
depicted as those who heed
God's commands while the
foolish ignore them.

Background and purpose
Proverbs is a collection of
practical, ethical precepts
about day-to-day living. They
are arranged in balanced pairs
of thoughts using contrasting
parallelism. Teaching with the
use of proverbs is one of the
world's most ancient methods
of instruction. Solomon's
writing cover a broad range of
topics, emphasizing correct
moral and religious behavior
that should be seen in God's
people.

Author
Solomon wrote most of the
proverbs in the book of
Proverbs. Solomon "spoke
three thousand proverbs and

his songs numbered a
thousand and five" *(1 Kings
4:32)*. Other authors in the
book of Proverbs are "the
sayings of the wise" *(22:17)*;
Agur *(30)*; and King Lemuel
(31:1-9).

Date
Solomon's proverbs would
have been written in the tenth
century BC.

Brief outline

1. Facets of wisdom *1:1–9:18*

2. Proverbs of Solomon
10:1–22:16; 25:1–29:27

3. Proverbs of wise men
22:17–24:34

4. Proverbs of Agur *30:1-33*

5. Proverbs of King Lemuel
31:1-9

6. The ideal wife *31:10-31*

Christ in Proverbs
- Jesus is the wisdom of God,
  see 1 Corinthians 1:30
- Jesus is "a friend who sticks
  closer than a brother" *(18:24)*.

Ecclesiastes
What is the meaning of life?

"Now all has been heard; here is the conclusion of the matter: Fear God and keep his commandments."
Ecclesiastes 12:13

Major theme
Ecclesiastes is the Bible's most philosophical book. Its perspective is human wisdom and thus has some verses which run counter to the general teaching of Scripture, such as, "A man can do nothing better than to eat and drink and find satisfaction in his work" *(2:24)*. The writer is pointing out the folly of human reasoning in order to focus on the only true satisfaction which is to be found in God.

Background and purpose
Ecclesiastes is sort of an Old Testament treatise for worldly people. It is as if the author is saying: "Let's see what life without God is like. Yes, life is indeed futile and miserable and meaningless, but life with God makes all the difference." Solomon shows the pointlessness of things that people commonly look to for happiness: human learning, politics, sensual delight, honor, powers, riches and possessions.

Author
The author of the book of Ecclesiastes calls himself *qoheleth*, the preacher. He also calls himself, "son of David, king of Jerusalem" *(1:1)*. This would appear to make it plain that Solomon wrote Ecclesiastes and this is the prevailing view.

Date
Assuming that Solomon was the author places the date of Ecclesiastes in the tenth century BC.

Brief outline

1. The theme: the emptiness of godless living *1:1-3*

2. This theme is demonstrated *1:4–3:22*

3. The problems of human life *4:1–6:12*

4. Coping in this life *7:1–12:8*

5. Conclusion: Fear God and keep his commands *12:9-14*

Christ in Ecclesiastes
• God has "set eternity in the hearts of men" and only Jesus can provide ultimate satisfaction and wisdom.

21

Song of Songs
The most beautiful of all songs

"Many waters cannot quench
   love;
rivers cannot wash it away."
Song of Songs 8:7

Major theme
No Bible book has been
interpreted in so many
different ways as the Song of
Songs. Most of the
interpretations fall into two
categories: literal or allegorical.

1. Allegorical
* The Jewish Talmud, the official
  teaching of Orthodox Jews,
  states that it is an allegory of
  God's love for Israel.
* Some Christian commentators
  extend this interpretation to say
  that it is an allegory of God's
  love for his people, the
  Christian Church.

2. Literal
* Theodore of Mopsuestia, 4th
  century, said that it was a love
  poem that Solomon wrote in
  honor of his marriage.
* Some Christian commentators
  extend this interpretation to
  say that it is a beautiful
  depiction of a married couple.

Background and purpose
The directly sensuous
language in this book has been
criticized. Some say this
represents the holy affections
that exist between God and his
people while others say that
this is a description of one of
God's gifts: the unashamed

appreciation of physical
attraction.

Author
Good arguments exist for
crediting Solomon as the
author of the Song of Songs as
the Talmud did. The book
opens with the words,
"Solomon's Song of Songs"
(1:1). Solomon is mentioned
seven times in the book.
"Look! It is Solomon's
carriage" *(3:7)*.

Date
Assuming that Solomon was
the author, the Song of Songs
was written in the 10th century
BC.

Brief outline

1. Affection between bride and
   bridegroom *1:1–3:5*

2. The bride accepts the
   bridegroom's invitation
   3:6–5:1

3. The bride's dream *5:2–6:3*

4. The bride and bridegroom
   express mutual love *6:4–8:14*

Christ in Song of Songs
* If the book is interpreted as a
  picture of the Christian church,
  the bridegroom is then taken to
  represent Jesus and the great
  love he has for every believer.

Isaiah
Salvation and the Servant

"For to us a child is born,
  to us a son is given,
    and the government will be
      on his shoulders.
And he will be called
  Wonderful Counselor, Mighty
    God, Everlasting Father,
    Prince of Peace."
  Isaiah 9:6

Major theme
Isaiah has a two-fold message:
condemnation *(1–39)* and
consolation *(40–66)*.

Background and purpose
Isaiah's prophecies and visions
came during the reigns of four
kings: Uzziah, Jotham, Ahaz
and Hezekiah. When Isaiah
started his prophecies Israel
was in the final stages of
collapse. The northern
kingdom had been captured by
Assyria and the southern
kingdom of Judah was heading
for a similar end. Isaiah
pronounces God's judgment
on the sins of Judah and then
the surrounding nations. But
Isaiah goes on to console
God's people with his message
of future restoration and hope.

Author
The author of the prophecy of
Isaiah is stated in the opening
verse. "The vision concerning

Judah and Jerusalem that
Isaiah son of Amoz saw ..."
(1:1)

Date
Isaiah lived in Jerusalem in the
second half of the eighth
century BC. Since most of the
events described in chapters
1–39 took place in Isaiah's
ministry, Isaiah probably wrote
these chapters shortly after 701
BC following the destruction of
the Assyrian army. The rest of
the book was written later on
in his life.

Brief outline

1. Messages of rebuke and
   promise *1:1–6:13*

2. Judgment and blessings on
   Judah *7:1–12:6*

3. Judgment on the other nations
   13:1–23:18

4. The apocalypse of Isaiah
   24:1–27:13

5. Judgment and blessing on
   Judah, Israel and Assyria
   28:1–39:8

6. Future blessing and comfort on
   Judah *40:1–66:24*

Christ in Isaiah
• Jesus is the Servant about whom
  Isaiah prophecies. The best
  known prophecies describe
  Christ's virgin birth *(Isaiah
  7:14)* and his sufferings *(ch. 53)*.

Jeremiah
"The weeping prophet"

"'The time is coming,' declares the Lord, 'when I will make a new covenant with the house of Israel.' ... 'I will put my law in their minds and write it on their hearts. I will be their God, and they will be my people.'"
Jeremiah 31:31,33

Major theme
Jeremiah's main message is one of impending judgment on the people of Jerusalem.

Background and purpose
Jeremiah's prophecies are God's final words of warning to the people in the final years before the destruction of Jerusalem. Jeremiah directed his prophecies to the people of Judah from 627 BC until the time of the fall of Jerusalem to King Nebuchadnezzar of Babylon in 586 BC. Jeremiah consistently prophesied that this would happen to Jerusalem. His message was unheeded. As a result he was persecuted, put in stocks, and even thrown into a cistern. With foreign powers constantly threatening Jerusalem, it's hard to understand why the preaching of Jeremiah was viewed with such contempt by the people of that generation.

Author
The book of Jeremiah bears its author's name. Jeremiah is called "the weeping prophet" because of the intense despair and loneliness he felt as the people rejected God and his words.

Date
The book of Jeremiah was written in the sixth century BC. It covers the three parts of Jeremiah's ministry:
- From 627–605 BC when he prophesied while Judah was threatened by Assyria and Egypt.
- From 605–586 BC when he prophesied while Judah was besieged by Babylon.
- From 586–580 BC when he ministered in Jerusalem and Egypt after Judah's downfall.

Brief outline

1. Prophecies against Judah
   1:1–25:38

2. Jeremiah's life *26:1–45:5*

3. Prophecies against foreign nations *46:1–51:64*

4. The fall of Jerusalem *52:1-34*

Christ in Jeremiah
- Jesus is the "Hope of Israel." *(14:8)*
- Jesus is our Potter *(18:6)*.
- Jesus is the "Shepherd" and "righteous Branch" *(23:3,5)*.

Lamentations
The book of tears

"They [the Lord's compassions]
  are new every morning;
  great is your faithfulness.
I say to myself, 'The Lord is my
  portion;
  therefore I will wait for him.'"
Lamentations 3:23-24

Major theme
The book is a sequel to the book of Jeremiah. It is a series of laments over the fallen Jerusalem.

Background and purpose
Each chapter of this book consists of one lamentation or elegy written in a special poetic form.

  Each lamentation has 22 sections and each section corresponds to a successive letter of the Hebrew alphabet (which has only 22 letters).

  The Septuagint introduces this book with the words: "And it came to pass after Israel was led into captivity that Jeremiah sat weeping and lamenting and lamented this lamentation over Jerusalem."

  The disastrous fall of Jerusalem in 587 BC needs to be explained. This book says that although the visible signs of God's presence in God's city and God's temple have been destroyed, God's people will be purified as a result.

Author
The author is not named, but tradition and the fact that Jeremiah was an eyewitness of the destruction of Jerusalem, makes Jeremiah the most likely author.

Date
Lamentations must have been written after the fall of Jerusalem in 586 BC, but before it was rebuilt and dedicated in 516 BC. The graphic laments place the time of writing close to the destruction of Jerusalem.

25

Brief outline

1. Jerusalem's sorrows *1:1-22*
2. Jerusalem's punishment *2:1-22*
3. Judah's hope in God's mercy *3:1-66*
4. Jerusalem: past and present *4:1-22*
5. A prayer for mercy *5:1-22*

Christ in Lamentations
• Jesus is seen as "my portion" *(3:24)*.

Ezekiel
The watchman's report

"'For I will take you out of the nations; I will gather you from all the countries and bring you back into your own land.'"
Ezekiel 36:24

Major theme
The book of Ezekiel shows God's faithfulness to Israel and all his holy people, and that God's purposes through judgment and blessing are the same: that his people may come to know that he is the Lord.

Background and purpose
Ezekiel the prophet was one of the Jewish exiles in Babylon during the last days of the kingdom of Judah. He was deported to Babylon in 597 BC along with King Jehoiachin and was relocated to the village of Tel Abib on the river Chebar. He announced God's judgment upon Judah and the surrounding countries. After the fall of Jerusalem he prophesied revival, restoration and a future for God's people.

Author
All that is known about the prophet Ezekiel comes from the prophecy which bears his name. More than any other prophet, he acted out the symbolism of his prophecies.

Date
The book of Ezekiel contains more dates than any other Old Testament prophetic book. Ezekiel received his call in July 593 BC, seven years before the destruction of Jerusalem. Ezekiel's last dated oracle came in April 571 BC, 15 years after the destruction of Jerusalem. It is assumed that Ezekiel wrote his prophecy around that time.

Brief outline

1. Ezekiel's call *1:1–3:27*

2. Prophecies of doom for Jerusalem *4:1–24:27*

3. God's judgment on the nations *25:1–32:32*

4. God's promise of renewal *33:1–37:28*

5. Prophecy against Gog *38:1–39:29*

6. Visions of the future temple and land *40:1–48:35*

Important events
Descriptions of:
- The departure of the glory of the Lord from the temple
- The fall of Jerusalem
- The return of God's glory

Christ in Ezekiel
- The caring, searching shepherd is a picture of Jesus. "'I will search for the lost and bring back the strays. I will bind up the injured and strengthen the weak ...'" *(34:16)*.

Daniel
The book of visions

"'In the time of those kings, the God of heaven will set up a kingdom that will never be destroyed, nor will it be left to another people. It will crush all those kingdoms and bring them to an end, but it will itself endure for ever.'" *Daniel 2:44*

Major theme
When God's people had little hope, Daniel provided encouragement by revealing God's power and his plans for the future.

Background and purpose
The book of Daniel records the experiences of Daniel and some of his fellow-exiles in Babylon and how their faith in God protected them. It has never been easy interpreting the visions about the rise and fall of several empires, in the second part of the book of Daniel. Jesus took seriously Daniel's prophecies about Antiochus Epiphanes, who ruled most of Asia Minor, Syria and Palestine from 175 BC until 164 BC. *See Matthew 24:15*

One helpful way of interpreting these prophecies is to see that they may have more than one point of fulfilment:
• In the time of Antiochus
• When the city of Jerusalem fell again in AD 70
• At the final End Time.

Author
Daniel is stated as the author of this book *(9:2)*. Jesus attributed the quotation from Daniel *(9:27)* to "the prophet Daniel" *(Matthew 24:15)*. Certain scholars do not accept Daniel as the author, nor do they accept prophetic predictions. Thus they date the book as late as 160 BC, which of course eliminates all the prophetic element of the book.

Date
Daniel prophesied in Babylon and probably completed his book just after Babylon was captured by Cyrus in 539 BC.

Brief outline

1. Daniel's life at the Babylonian court *1:1–2:49*

2. Daniel's early visions in Babylon *3:1–6:28*

3. Daniel's visions of world empires *7:1–8:27*

4. Daniel's prayer and vision of the 70 "sevens" *9:1-27*

5. Daniel's visions of Israel's future *10:1–12:13*

Important events
• Daniel's three friends survive being thrown into the fiery furnace
• Daniel in the lions' den

Christ in Daniel
• The "Ancient of Days" is Jesus *(7:13)*.

Hosea
The book for backsliders

"'My people are determined to
    turn from me.
Even if they call to the Most
    High,
he will by no means exalt them.
'How can I give you up, Ephraim?
    How can I hand you over,
    Israel?'"
Hosea 11:7-8

Major themes
Apostasy from God is spiritual
adultery. The Lord loves Israel
despite her sin. The tone of the
book is filled with God's
mercy, loyalty, devotion and
unconditional love.

Background and purpose
Hosea had a tragic family life.
God told him to marry Gomer
but she proved unfaithful to
Hosea, ran away and became a
prostitute. Hosea continued to
love her, bought her back
(even though she was little
more than a slave) and
restored her to being his wife.

  The prophet Hosea takes his
own marriage as a picture of
the relationship between God
and Israel. God loved Israel,
even when she was unfaithful
to him.

Author
Hosea was a prophet to the
northern kingdom of Israel for
about 50 years and the book
that bears his name is filled
with his prophecies.

Date
Hosea prophesied in the
middle of the eighth century
BC.

Brief outline

1. Hosea's family *1:1–3:5*	
2. Israel's corruption *4:1–5:15*	
3. God's love is rejected *6:1–8:6*	
4. Judgment will come *8:7–10:15*	
5. Repentance is possible *11:1–14:9*	

Christ in Hosea
• Christ's loving, redemptive work
  on our behalf is mirrored in
  Hosea's love and restoration of
  Gomer.

Joel
Judgment and mercy

"'And afterwards,
  I will pour our my Spirit on all
    people.
Your sons and daughters will
    prophesy,
  your old men will dream
    dreams,
  your young men will see
    visions.'"
Joel 2:28

Major theme
The key theme in the book of Joel is the day of the Lord or the day of judgment when God directly intervenes in human history. Only a change of heart and a change of life will bring restoration and blessing.

Background and purpose
A recent plague of locusts is taken by Joel to signify divine judgment on Judah's sins. Judah was now surrounded by enemy nations who were like hordes of locusts. Judah's only hope of survival was to repent and seek God's mercy.

The Spirit of God promised in *(2:28-31)* was fulfilled on the Day of Pentecost *(Acts 2:1-20)*.

Author
Joel, the son of Pethuel, was a prophet to the southern kingdom of Judah. Nothing is known about Joel outside his prophecy. There are twelve other people called Joel in the Old Testament, but the prophet Joel is linked to none of them.

Date
The book does not have any explicit time references in it and so cannot be precisely dated. Many conservative scholars suggest that Joel was written in the ninth or eighth century BC.

Brief outline

1. The plague of locusts
   1:1-20

2. Apocalyptic judgment threatened *2:1-27*

3. The outpouring of the Spirit *2:28-32*

4. The oppressor will be judged *3:1-16*

5. Restoration of God's people *3:17-21*

29

Christ in Joel
- Jesus is a "refuge for his people" *(3:16)*.

Amos
Prophet to the affluent society

"Seek good, not evil,
   that you may live.
Then the Almighty will be with
   you,
   just as you say he is."
   Amos 5:14

Major theme
God is just. He
demands social
justice and must
judge sin.

Background and purpose
Amos accused Israel of
neglecting the worship of God
and indulging in extravagant
luxury. Rich merchants
oppressed the poor and
worshiped the pagan idols that
Jeroboam I had introduced.
Israel was enjoying great
prosperity and commanded a
strong political and military
position. But Amos warned
Israel of God's impending
judgment. The proportion of
teaching about God's
judgment compared to hope is
higher in Amos than in any
other prophet. However, Amos
ends his book on a note of
hope:
"'I will plant Israel in their own
   land,
   never again to be uprooted
from the land I have given
   them,'
   says the Lord." *9:15*

Author
Amos was a sheep farmer from
"Tekoa" *(1:1)*, a small town
six miles south of Bethlehem,
in the southern kingdom of
Judah, yet he prophesied to
the northern kingdom of
Israel. The only Old
Testament appearance of
the name "Amos" is in
this book.

Date
Amos prophesied "when
Uzziah was king of Judah
[792–740 BC] and Jeroboam
son of Jehoash was king of
Israel [793–753 BC]" *(1:1)*.
Amos probably prophesied
around 760–750 BC.

Brief outline

1.	Prophecies against the nations *1:3–2:16*
2.	The corrupt land *3:1–6:14*
3.	Visions of doom *7:1–8:3*
4.	Judgment day *8:4–9:10*
5.	Promised restoration *9:11-15*

Christ in Amos
• Jesus is the Restorer of his
people *(9:11-15)*.

Obadiah
God's judgment is certain

> "Deliverers will go up on Mount Zion
>   to govern the mountains of Esau.
>   And the kingdom will be the Lord's."
> *Obadiah 21*

Major theme
Sure retribution must overtake merciless pride. God will punish those who refuse to live justly and righteously.

Background and purpose
Obadiah's prophecy is aimed at the Edomites who are judged by God for their inhumanity to Israel in the day of its suffering. "'Because of the violence against your brother Jacob, you will be covered with shame; you will be destroyed for ever'" *(10)*. The Edomites refused to allow Israel to travel through their country *(Numbers 20:14-21)*, and they rejoiced when Jerusalem was captured *(Psalm 137:7)*. Edom's crimes are listed in order of their ascending horror *(11-14)*.

Obadiah has one of the most realistic descriptions of the siege and attack of a city in the whole of the Old Testament.

Author
Nothing is known about Obadiah outside his prophecy. We are not told the name of his father or where he was born. His name means "servant of the Lord" and was a common one in the Old Testament.

Date
If verses 11-14 refer to the Babylonian attacks on Jerusalem in 605–586 BC that would mean that Obadiah was a contemporary of Jeremiah and this gives a sixth century BC date for the writing of Obadiah.

Brief outline

1. Edom's fall is prophecied *1-9*

2. Edom's sins exposed *10-14*

Christ in Obadiah
- Jesus is the Judge of the nations *(15-16)*, and the Savior of Israel *(17-20)*.

Jonah
Can God bless the wicked?

"'Go to the great city of Nineveh and proclaim to it the message I give you.'"
Jonah 3:2

Major theme
Jonah reveals God's concern for all people as he shows the power of God over nature *(1–2)*, and the mercy of God in human affairs *(3–4)*.

Background and purpose
Some interpret the whole book of Jonah as a parable rather than as actual fact.

Arguments in favor of treating Jonah as an historical event are:
• Jonah is described as a real person.
• Jesus took Jonah and his adventures seriously and even compared his own resurrection to Jonah's experience inside the fish *(Matthew 12:39-41)*.

The Hebrew idiom about the time Jonah was inside the fish, "three days and three nights" *(1:17)* only requires a part of the first and third days.

Author
The book does not identify the author, but it is traditionally ascribed to Jonah.

Date
A wide range of dates for the writing of Jonah have been proposed, from the days of Elijah and Elisha in the ninth century BC to the third century when it has been reduced to an historical fiction by some commentators. If Jonah was a contemporary of Amos there are good reasons for suggesting that Jonah was written in the eighth century BC.

Brief outline
1. God commissions Jonah to preach against Nineveh, but Jonah takes a boat destined for "Tarshish" *(1:3)* in the opposite direction. The Lord saves pagan sailors from being shipwrecked *1:1-17*

2. The Lord rescues disobedient Jonah from drowning by the timely arrival of a huge fish *2:1-11*

3. The Lord saves repentant Nineveh *3:1-10*

4. Jonah learns to look beyond his own nation and to trust the Creator of all people *4:1-11*

Christ in Jonah
• Jonah's experience is a "type" of the death, burial, and resurrection of Jesus *(Matthew 12:39-41)*.
• The Bible does not mention a whale, but a "great fish" (King James Version), or a "huge fish" *(Matthew 12:40)*.

32

Micah
Judgment and hope

"He has showed you, O man,
    what is good.
  And what does the Lord
    require of you?
To act justly and to love mercy
  and to walk humbly with your
    God."
Micah 6:8

Major theme
The focus is on God's hatred
of sin, but also his promise to
rescue those who would
change their hearts and
actions. The Bethlehem-born
Messiah will be humankind's
deliverer.

Background and purpose
The book of Micah is a
collection of speeches. Micah
forecasts about God's
impending judgment on
Judah's sins *(chapters 1–3)*, and
graphically describes both their
sins and punishment. Micah
goes on to prophesy a bright
future after this judgment
(chapters 4–5). The concluding
two chapters are in the form of
the Lord's controversy with his
people and the mercy he finally
has on them.

Author
Micah was a prophet to the
southern kingdom of Judah.
He is mentioned in Jeremiah
26:18, "Micah of Moresheth
[in southern Judah] prophesied
in the days of Hezekiah king of
Judah." Apart from that and

what we learn about him from
the book of Micah we know
nothing about him.

Date
We ascertain from the opening
verse of Micah that the
prophet prophesied during the
reigns of Jotham, Ahaz and
Hezekiah. This makes Micah a
contemporary of the prophet
Isaiah. Micah must have
prophesied between 750 BC
and 686 BC.

Brief outline

1. Judgment against Israel and
   Judah *1:1–3:12*

2. Hope for Israel and Judah
   4:1–5:15

3. God's case against Israel *6:1-16*

4. Micah's sad poem and a
   hopeful future *7:1-20*

Christ in Micah
• Micah contains one of the
  clearest and most important
  prophecies about Jesus:
"'But you, Bethlehem Ephrathah,
  though you are small among
    the clans of Judah,
out of you will come for me
  one who will be ruler over
    Israel,
whose origins are from of old,
  from ancient times.'"
Micah 5:2

Nahum
The fall of Nineveh

*"The Lord is good,
a refuge in times of trouble."*
Nahum 1:7

Major theme
God is good, but God's judgment is to engulf wicked Nineveh.

Background and purpose
God's followers in Judah would be comforted to learn about God's judgment on the brutal Assyrians. Nahum announces that the Assyrians are doomed because of their excessive pride, idolatry and oppression. The book affirms God's active interest in all nations, not just Israel.

Author
Nahum is only mentioned in the opening verse of the prophecy which bears his name. "An oracle concerning Nineveh. The book of the vision of Nahum the Elkoshite" *(1:1)*. Even the location of Elkosh is not known.

Date
Nahum pictures the fall of Nineveh to the Babylonians in 612 BC as a future event. Nahum also refers to the fall of Thebes (663 BC) as an event that had already happened: "Are you better than Thebes ... Yet she was taken captive" *(3:8,10)*. As Nahum pictures the fall of Nineveh as an imminent event, it is likely that the book of Nahum was much closer to 612 BC than to 663 BC. This would make Nahum a contemporary of Zephaniah.

Brief outline

1. Nahum announces the coming of the divine avenger on Nineveh *1:1-15*

2. Nahum gives a detailed description of the sieges, fall and sacking of Nineveh *2:1-13*

3. Using horrific language, Nahum pronounces, "Woe to the city of blood" *3:1-19*

Christ in Nahum
• "... the feet of one who brings good news, who proclaims peace!' is applied to the message and ministry of Jesus. *See Isaiah 52:7 and Romans 10:15*

Habakkuk
Can God use the wicked?

"'See, he is puffed up;
his desires are not upright–
but the righteous will live by his
faith–...'"
Habakkuk 2:4

Major theme
Justification by faith is God's way of salvation. God is just and he is still in control.

Background and purpose
Habakkuk wrestles with a profound and perplexing theological problem: "How can God's patience with evil conform with his holiness?"

The answer provided by the book of Habakkuk is that God is sovereign and thus deals with the wicked in his own way, in his own time.

Paul quotes Habakkuk 2:4 in Romans 1. It was this verse that profoundly influenced Martin Luther and led to the Protestant reformation.

Author
All we know about Habakkuk is that he was a prophet.

Date
The only explicit time reference in Habakkuk is to the impending Babylonian invasion *(1:6; 2:1; 3:16)*. "I am raising up the Babylonians, that ruthless and impetuous people, who sweep across the whole earth to seize dwelling-places not their own" *(1:6)*. Since the Babylonians won a decisive victory at Carchemish in 605 BC, the prophecy of Habakkuk was probably at this time.

Brief outline

1. Habakkuk argues with God *1:2-4*

2. God replies *1:5-11*

3. Habakkuk protests *1:12-17*

4. God replies *2:1-20*

5. God's judgment and salvation *3:1-16*

6. The confidence of the godly *3:7-19*

Christ in Habakkuk
- "I will be joyful in God my Savior" *(3:18)*. Jesus, the root of whose name means "salvation", is "the Savior of the world" *(John 4:42)*.

Zephaniah
A warning of judgment

"Seek the Lord, all you humble of
the land,
   you who do what he
   commands.
Seek righteousness, seek humility;
   perhaps you will be sheltered
   on the day of the Lord's anger."
   Zephaniah 2:3

Major theme

God's judgment must precede
kingdom blessing. Seek the
Lord now!

Background and purpose

Zephaniah prophesies a
universal judgment which will
begin with Judah, but ends
with a promise of restoration.
He states that their sins are the
reason for God's punishment
of their nation. He also makes
it clean that God will be
merciful toward the Israelites.

Author

According to the opening verse
of this prophecy Zephaniah
was the great, great, great
grandson of King Hezekiah, a
notable king of Judah. We are
not given any other informa-
tion about Zephaniah's
background, but from his
prophecy we learn that he was
fully acquainted with the
current political issues and
with court circles.

Date

"The word of the Lord came to
Zephaniah son of Cushi, the son
of Gedaliah, the son of Amariah,
the son of Hezekiah, during the
reign of Josiah son of Amon king
of Judah." *1:1*

Since King Josiah reigned
640–609 BC, we know the
dates of Zephaniah's prophetic
ministry.

Brief outline

1. God's judgment is announced
   1:1-18

2. Judah is told to repent. *2:1-3*

3. God's judgment on other
   nations *2:4-15*

4. Judah will not escape God's
   judgment *3:1-8*

5. God promises to restore a
   remnant *3:9-20*

Christ in Zephaniah

- Jesus fulfils the promise of
  (3:17):
   "'The Lord your God is with
   you,
   he will quiet you with his love,
   he will rejoice over you with
   singing.'"

Haggai
Building for God

"This is what the Lord Almighty says: 'Give careful thought to your ways. Go up into the mountains and bring down timber and build the house, so that I may take pleasure in it and be honored,' says the Lord."
Haggai 1:7-8

Major theme
The Lord's temple and worship deserve top priority. God must have just place in a person's life.

Background and purpose
Haggai's prophecies help us to understand some of the problems of the returning Jews. Haggai rebukes them for their neglecting their work for God and concentrating their efforts on their own prosperity, rather than first rebuilding the temple and re-establishing the priestly offerings.

Author
Haggai was a prophet to the Jews who returned to Jerusalem from Babylonia.

Date
This book has five separate prophecies which are all dated. The first prophecy was "In the second year of King Darius, on the first day of the sixth month" *(1:1)*. This can be related to our modern calendar and is August 19, 520 BC. All Haggai's prophecies come during a four-month period in 520 BC.

Brief outline

1. **First prophecy** Haggai urges that work be started on the rebuilding of the temple *1:1-11*

2. **Second prophecy** Haggai encourages the Jews in their work *1:12-15*

3. **Third prophecy** Another message of encouragement from Haggai *2:1-9*

4. **Fourth prophecy** Present blessings are promised *2:10-19*

5. **Fifth prophecy** Haggai gives a personal message to Zerubbabel *2:20-23*

Christ in Haggai
- Jesus is portrayed in Zerubbabel. "'I will take you, my servant Zerubbabel ... and I will make you like my signet ring, for I have chosen you ...'" *(2:23)*

Zechariah
Prepare for the Messiah

"'Therefore tell the people: This is what the Lord Almighty says: "Return to me," declares the Lord Almighty, "and I will return to you."'" *Zechariah 1:3*

Major theme
The Lord will remember his people Israel and will show the eventual holiness of Jerusalem and her people. The book gives the assurance that God is in control at all times.

Background and purpose
Zechariah, a contemporary of Haggai, tells the Jews who returned to Jerusalem from Babylonia to complete the rebuilding of the temple. The motivation Zechariah gives for this is that the temple has always been central to Israel's spiritual heritage and that it is closely linked to the coming of the Messiah.

The book of Zechariah contains a series of eight visions *(1–8)*, four messages *(7–8)*, and two burdens *(9–14)* which convey some of the clearest prophecies in Scripture about the coming Messiah.

Author
Zechariah was a priest as well as a prophet, being the son of Berekiah and grandson of Iddo *(1:1)*. He was born in Babylonia and brought to Palestine when the Jewish exiles returned under Zerubbabel and Joshua the high priest.

Date
Zechariah was a contemporary of Haggai the prophet, Zerubbabel the governor and Joshua the high priest. Haggai started preaching in 520 BC, but his final prophecy *(chapters 9–14)*, were probably not delivered until after 480 BC.

Brief outline

1. A call to repentance *1:1-6*	
2. A series of eight night visions *1:7–6:8*	
3. The crowning of Joshua *6:9-15*	
4. The question of fasting *7:1-3*	
5. Four messages of Zechariah *7:4–8:23*	
6. Two burdens of Zechariah *9:1–14:21*	

Christ in Zechariah
Jesus is seen as
- The Branch *(3:8)*.
- The priest on his throne (King-Priest) *(6:13)*.
- The Shepherd *(13:7)*.

Malachi
God's love for his faithless people

"'But for you who revere my name, the sun of righteousness will rise with healing in its wings. And you will go out and leap like calves released from the stall.'"
Malachi 4:2

Major theme
Let the wicked be warned about the certainty of judgment, but God will love and bless his people as they turn to him.

Background and purpose
The Lord is seen having a dialogue with his people. "But you ask," is contrasted with, "This is what the Almighty says."

> **Question, for which God has good answers**

- "'How have you loved us?'" *1:2-5*
- "'How have we shown contempt for your name?'" *1:6–2:9*
- "'Why do we profane the covenant?'" *2:10-16*
- "'How have we wearied him?'" *2:17–3:6*
- "'How are we to return?'" *3:7-12*
- "'What have we said against you?'" *3:13–4:3*

Author
Malachi is only mentioned in the Old Testament in the opening verse of the prophecy which bears his name. The book of Malachi is traditionally attributed to him.

Date
Malachi's prophecies, like those of Haggai and Zechariah, were addressed to the restored community of Israel, around 450 BC and 425 BC. Malachi's prophecies are the last of the Old Testament prophecies in the Bible. After Malachi no prophetic voice was heard until the coming of John the Baptist.

Brief outline

1. The Lord's love for Israel *1:2-5*

2. The priests are rebuked *1:6–2:9*

3. Israel's faithlessness in worship and marriage *2:10-16*

4. The day of the Lord's justice *2:17–3:5*

5. The Lord's blessing on giving *3:6-12*

6. The righteous are vindicated in the day of the Lord *3:13–4:6*

Christ in Malachi
- Jesus is the messenger of God's covenant. "Then the Lord you are seeking will come to his temple; the messenger of the covenant, whom you desire, will come" *(3:1)*.
- Jesus is the "sun of righteousness" *(4:2)*.

Matthew
Jesus, the promised King

"'All authority in heaven and on earth has been given to me. Therefore go and make disciples of all nations, baptizing them in the name of the Father and of the Son and of the Holy Spirit, and teaching them to obey everything I have commanded you. And surely I am with you always, to the very end of the age.'"
Matthew 28:18-20

Major theme
Matthew wrote this account of Jesus' life to convince the Jews that Jesus was their Messiah.

Background and purpose
Matthew wrote his Gospel to show the links between the Old Testament and Jesus, to record the wealth of teaching Jesus gave to his disciples, to set out how Jesus expected his followers to behave, to answer some of the questions raised by members of the church, (such as the early life of Jesus and when he would return) and to say how the church should be run.

Author
Matthew. One of Jesus' twelve apostles, the former tax-collector, who was also known as Levi. When he became a follower of Jesus he abandoned everything and held a feast in his house for Jesus and other tax-collectors and "sinners".

Date
Probably written between AD 60–65 before the fall of the city of Jerusalem in AD 70.

Brief outline
1. Genealogy and birth of Jesus Christ *1:1–2:23*

2. John the Baptist's ministry *3:1-12*

3. Jesus' baptism and temptations *3:13–4:11*

4. Jesus' public ministry in Galilee *4:12–18:35*

5. From Galilee to Jerusalem *19:1–20:34*

6. Jesus' last week *21:1–27:66*

7. The resurrection and appearances of Jesus *28:1-20*

Keys to Matthew
- **Key word** Kingdom
- **Key chapter 12**, in which the Pharisees reject Jesus as Messiah of the nation of Israel.
- Matthew stresses Jesus' exhortations to his followers and so this book has always had a strong appeal to new Christians. 60% of Matthew's Gospel, that is 644 verses out of the total of 1,071 verses, contain the spoken words of Jesus.
- Matthew has 53 quotations from the Old Testament and 76 allusions from the Old Testament.

40

Mark
Jesus, the obedient Servant

"'For even the Son of Man did not come to be served, but to serve, and to give his life as a ransom for many.'" *Mark 10:45*

Major theme
Through the example of Jesus, Mark demonstrates the service and sacrifice of the Messiah that Jesus is continually serving and doing.

Background and purpose
Mark's Gospel is a short book. It does not give a full account of Christ's sermons but focuses on Christ's miracles. Mark presents the person and work of Jesus Christ to a primarily, non-Jewish audience, possibly those experiencing persecution in Rome.

Author
John Mark.

Mark and his cousin, Barnabas, accompanied Paul on his first missionary journey *(Acts 13:5)*. Mark deserted the missionaries at Perga, so Paul refused to take Mark on a second journey. Instead, Mark went with Barnabas to Cyprus. Later he was reconciled to Paul *(Colossians 4:10)* and was closely associated with Peter *(1 Peter 5:13)*.

Date
Between AD 55 and the early 60s. Tradition suggests Mark wrote this Gospel under the direction of Peter.

Brief outline

1. Jesus begins his public ministry *1:1-20*

2. Jesus' public ministry in Galilee *1:21–6:29*

3. Jesus withdraws from Galilee *6:30–9:50*

4. Jesus' ministry in Perea *10:1-52*

5. Jesus' last week *11:1–15:47*

6. Jesus comes back to life and his ascension *16:1-20*

Keys to Mark

- **Key word** The Greek word *euthus* (immediately or at once) occurs 42 times. Mark seems to hurry the reader on from one amazing story to the next.

- **Key chapter 8**, which shows a change of emphasis in Jesus' ministry. After Peter confesses, "You are the Christ" *(8:29)*, Jesus teaches his disciples about his sacrificial death.

- 42% of Mark's Gospel, that is 285 verses out of the total of 678 verses, contain the spoken words of Jesus.

- Mark has 36 quotations from the Old Testament and 27 allusions from the Old Testament.

Luke
Jesus, the perfect Man

"Therefore, since I myself have carefully investigated everything from the beginning, it seemed good also to me to write an orderly account for you, most excellent Theophilus, so that you may know the certainty of the things you have been taught."
Luke 1:3-4

Major theme
Luke wanted to show that Jesus was Savior for all types of people and not just an elite group. Jesus is pictured showing more interest in children, women and social outcasts than in the other Gospels.

Background and purpose
Luke is the only Gospel writer to spell out at length why he wrote his Gospel. See *Luke 1:1-4*

Luke stresses the humanity of Jesus and so writes in detail about his ancestry and birth.

Author
Luke, a Greek-speaking doctor, was Paul's faithful friend. He was a Gentile and a traveling companion of Paul *(Philemon 24)*, who remained with the apostle even when he was imprisoned late in life *(2 Tim 4:11)* Luke also wrote Acts.

Date
Most scholars accept between AD 60 and 65.

Brief outline
1. Prologue *1:1-4*

2. Birth and childhood of John the Baptist and Jesus *1:5–2:52*

3. John the Baptist's ministry *3:1-20*

4. Jesus' baptism and temptations *3:21–4:13*

5. Jesus' public ministry in Galilee *4:14–9:50*

6. From Galilee to Jerusalem *9:51–19:27*

7. Jesus' last week *19:28–23:56*

8. Jesus' resurrection, appearances and ascension *24:1-53*

Keys to Luke
- **Key word** Seek.
- **Key chapter 15**, with its three parables illustrating that God through Jesus came to seek and to save the lost.
- **Key teaching** The parables of Jesus. Luke's portrait of Jesus uses more material than the other three Gospels.
- 16 of the 26 parables of Jesus recorded by Luke are found only in Luke's Gospel.
- 50% of Luke's Gospel, that is 586 verses out of the total of 1,151 verses, contain the spoken words of Jesus.
- Luke has 25 quotations from the Old Testament and 42 allusions from the Old Testament.

John
Jesus, the divine Son

"For God so loved the world that he gave his one and only Son, that whoever believes in him shall not perish but have eternal life."
John 3:16

Major theme
John's Gospel is no mere biography. It is a carefully-prepared Gospel treatise in which he selects evidence so his readers may believe that Jesus is the Christ.

Background and purpose
At the end of his Gospel, John tells his readers why he wrote it. See *John 20:30-31*

Much of John's teaching about Jesus is presented in the form of the different conversations people had with Jesus. John brings forward witness after witness who have had encounters with Jesus so that the reader has to make a decision about Jesus.

Author
The apostle John. John, a fisherman and son of Zebedee, was one Jesus' inner circle of three very close apostles; along with his brother, James. They were given the nickname the "sons of thunder". John, who leaned on Jesus at the Last Supper, was Jesus' closest friend. John never mentions himself by name in his Gospel, but uses the words "the disciple Jesus loved" instead.

Date
Approximately AD 90, probably the last of the Gospels to have been written.

Brief outline
1. Prologue *1:1-18*
2. Jesus' ministry in Galilee *1:19–12:50*
3. Jesus and the Last Supper *13:1–14:31*
4. Jesus' discourses as he goes to Gethsemane *15:1–16:33*
5. Jesus' prayer for his own *17:1-26*
6. Jesus' arrest, trial and crucifixion *18:1–19:42*
7. Jesus' resurrection and appearances *20:1–21:25*

Keys to John
- **Key word** Believe, nearly 100 times.
- John stresses the deity of the incarnate Son of God with his: seven "I am" statements *(6:35; 8:12; 10:7; 10:11; 11:25; 14:6; 15:1)*
- Seven miraculous signs *(1–12)*
- Five witnesses *(5:30-40)*
- 50% of John's Gospel, that is 419 verses out of the total of 879 verses, contain the spoken words of Jesus.
- John has 20 quotations and 105 allusions from the Old Testament.

43

Acts
The witnessing Church

"'But you will receive power when the Holy Spirit comes on you; and you will be my witnesses in Jerusalem, and in all Judea and Samaria, and to the ends of the earth.'" *Acts 1:8*

Major theme

Acts is Luke's sequel to his gospel and is an accurate account of the spread of the early Church under the guidance and empowering of the Holy Spirit. Luke records the spread of the Gospel from the ascension of Jesus to Paul's imprisonment in Rome – the center of the Roman Empire.

Background and purpose

The book is written to Theophilus, the same person to whom Luke's Gospel is addressed and presumably for the same purpose: to present an orderly account of historical facts to Theophilus (*Luke 1:1-4*). Basically, the book is written to confirm the faith of believers. It is the history of the apostles and covers approximately the first 30 years of the early Church.

Author

Luke. Luke, the writer of the gospel which bears his name accompanied the apostle Paul on some of his journeys, and recorded what happened in the book of Acts. Luke sailed to Rome with Paul, staying with him while he was a prisoner in the imperial capital.

Date

This book was apparently written in a two-year period after Paul's imprisonment in Rome, about AD 63, but before Paul's death (Acts 28:30). No outcome of Paul's trial is mentioned by Luke; nor is there any mention of the destruction of Jerusalem in AD 70. Therefore, a date in the early 60s is probable.

Brief outline

1. Peter and the beginning of the church in Jerusalem *1:1–2:47*

2. The ministry of Peter, Stephen, Barnabas and others *3:1–8:40*

3. Paul's conversion *9:1-31*

4. Peter's continuing ministry and the non-Jewish church *10:1–12:24*

5. Paul's missionary journeys *12:25–21:26*

6. Paul's imprisonment, trip to Rome and defense *21:27–28:31*

Keys to Acts

Key word Witness, coming more than 30 times.

Key chapter Chapter 2, which records the life-changing events of the Day of Pentecost.

Key teaching Acts describes the work of the Holy Spirit in the lives of the apostles and how God brought the Gentiles into the early church.

Romans
The heart of the Gospel

"I am not ashamed of the gospel, because it is the power of God for the salvation of everyone who believes; first for the Jew, then for the Gentiles. For in the gospel a righteousness from God is revealed, a righteousness that is by faith from first to last, just as it is written: 'The righteous will live by faith.'" *Romans 1:16-17*

Major theme
Romans, the first great work of Christian theology, is the most influential of all Paul's letters. It shows how helpless humanity can be delivered in Jesus.

Background and purpose
Paul longed to visit the Christians in Rome, the capital of the known world. This letter prepares the way for his visit. It is probable that some people had been criticizing his teaching. This gave him the opportunity to put down a summary of the good news about Jesus in greater detail than anywhere else in the New Testament. Included in this discussion are statements on righteousness and how it is obtained, God's justification and what makes it possible, holiness and how God accomplishes it in the lives of his people, Israel's rejection of the Messiah and its meaning

for Jew and non-Jew. The last five chapters are an encouragement to live the Christian life.

Author
The apostle Paul. The great apostle and pioneering missionary, whose letters form a large part of the New Testament.

Date
Paul dictated this letter to his friend Tertius around AD 57 in Corinth:
"I, Tertius, who wrote down this letter, greet you in the Lord." *Romans 16:22*

Brief outline

1. Greetings *1:1-7*
2. All the world is sinful *1:8–3:20*
3. The fact of salvation *3:21–5:21*
4. Salvation applied *6:1–8:39*
5. What about the Jews? *9:1–11:36*
6. Guidelines for the believer *12:1–15:33*
7. Closing greetings *16:1-27*

Keys to Romans
Key word Righteousness, used 62 times.
- When Christians rediscovered the book of Romans at the time of the Reformation the Christian Church was revitalized.

1 Corinthians
Dealing with a divided church

"Do you not know that your body is a temple of the Holy Spirit, who is in you, whom you have received from God? You are not your own; you were brought at a price. Therefore honor God with your body." 1 Corinthians 6:19-20

Major theme
Paul writes this letter to the church he had founded in hope of resolving the many problems that had arisen among the new Christians at Corinth – problems of division and Christian conduct.

Background and purpose
1 Corinthians is like listening to only one end of telephone conversation. It answers the following questions:

• How should we view church leaders?
• How should church discipline be carried out?
• Is it right for a Christian to take a fellow Christian to court?
• What does it mean to be free as a Christian?
• What are the spiritual gifts and which are the most important ones?
• What happens after we die?

Author
The apostle Paul. Paul was probably at Ephesus *(16:8)*, when Stephanus and two friends arrived with a letter from the Christians at Corinth: "I was glad when Stephanus,

Fortunatus and Achaicus arrived, because they have supplied what was lacking from you" *(16:18)*. This letter apparently requested Paul's judgment on certain issues: "Now for the matters you wrote about ..." *(7:1)*. Paul penned this letter to answer these questions.

Date
c. AD 54–55

Brief outline

1. The scandal of a divided church *1:1–4:21*

2. The scandal of immorality *5:1–6:20*

3. Questions about marriage *7:1-40*

4. Christian freedom *8:1–11:1*

5. Order in church services *11:2–14:40*

6. The resurrection of Jesus and believers *15:1-58*

7. Closing greetings *16:1-24*

Key to 1 Corinthians
• Corinth was infamous for its paganism and immorality. The term *Korinthiazomai* (to act like a Corinthian) was synonymous with debauchery and prostitution. *See 5:1-2.*
• **Key teaching** The church, spiritual gifts, and evidence for and implications of Jesus' resurrection.

2 Corinthians
Paul reveals his minister's heart

"Therefore, if anyone is in Christ, he is a new creation; the old has gone, the new has come!"
2 Corinthians 5:17

Major theme
Paul wrote 2 Corinthians in response to strong attacks which some Christians at Corinth had made on his person, motive and character.

Background and purpose
False apostles had moved in among the Christians at Corinth *(11:12-15)*. These "super-apostles" *(11:5)*, taught a different gospel *(11:12-15)*, and defied Paul's authority. The Christians at Corinth had, or were on the verge of, changing their minds about Paul. Paul wrote 2 Corinthians to tell them just how much this change of mind meant to him.

His letter warns them not to be too harsh with his opponents *(2:5-11)*; not to be closely linked with unbelievers *(6:14)*; to give generously to the collection of money being made for the poor Christians in Jerusalem *(8–9)*; how to deal with false teachers *(11:1-6)*; and concludes with Paul's happiness that the Corinthians have stopped following false teachers *(11:12-15)*.

Author
The apostle Paul.

Date
We know the precise date that Paul was originally in Corinth. It was when Gallio was proconsul in Achaia: "Paul left Athens and went to Corinth. ... While Gallio was proconsul of Achaia, the Jews made a united attack on Paul and brought him into court" *(Acts 18:1,12)*. This was in AD 51 or 52. So his first letter to Corinth must have been written in about AD 54–55 and his second letter about one year later in AD 55–56.

Brief outline

1. Introduction *1:1-11*

2. Why Paul changed his plans *1:12–2:13*

3. Paul's ministry *2:14–6:10*

4. Paul's instructions *6:11–9:15*

5. Paul defends his apostleship *10:1–12:14*

6. Closing remarks and farewell greetings *12:20–13:13*

Keys to 2 Corinthians
- It is full of autobiographical material.
- It is one of Paul's most personal letters.
- It has many personal anecdotes into Paul's personal life.

Galatians
The true Gospel

"It is for freedom that Christ has set us free. Stand firm, then, and do not let yourselves be burdened again by a yoke of slavery."
Galatians 5:1

Major theme
To show that faith and faith alone is the only ground for justification and good living *(2:16,22)*.

Major theme
Some Jewish Christians arrived in Galatia and were undermining Paul's teaching. The letter to the Galatians was Paul's response that Jesus brings freedom from the law.

Background and purpose
Galatians has been called the "Magna Charter of Christian freedom," as it has freed countless Christians, notably Martin Luther, from various forms of outward observance which have endangered the freedom of the gospel.

Paul knew what it was to live under the law and he saw that the gospel of grace was at stake if the new Christians tried to fulfil the requirements of the Mosaic Law. So, with great passion, he wrote this, his most "severe" letter to the Christians at Galatia.

Paul's purpose is to counteract the false teaching that was blending Jewish rituals and the Christian faith. Paul urges the Galatians to remain in the freedom they have in Christ but also cautions against the abuse of this freedom.

Author
The apostle Paul.

Date
This is probably the earliest letter Paul wrote – approximately AD 48. Other scholars suggest a date of AD 56.

Brief outline

1. Introduction *1:1-5*

2. Paul's defense of his apostolic authority *1:6–2:14*

3. Justification by faith *2:15–4:31*

4. Christian freedom and responsibility *5:1–6:10*

5. Conclusion *6:10-18*

Keys to Galatians
- It is a fighting letter. Paul uses strong language to make his point. "If anyone is preaching to you a gospel other than what you accepted, let him be eternally condemned!" *1:9*
- It is a loving letter. It reveals the care and concern of a great pastor. *4:19-20*

Ephesians
The letter of fullness

"Praise be to the God and Father of our Lord Jesus Christ, who has blessed us in the heavenly realms with every spiritual blessing in Christ." *Ephesians 1:3*

Major theme
There are two primary themes: God's grace and the unity of the body, the Church.

Background and purpose
Chapters 1–3 list the believer's heavenly possessions: adoption, citizenship, grace, inheritance, life, power and redemption.

Chapters 4–6 have 35 directives which instruct the believer about living the Christian life.

Paul made at least three visits to Ephesus, and lived there for three years teaching the new Christians and laying a firm spiritual foundation. Perhaps that is why this book does not address any specific error or false doctrine. Rather, the letter to the Ephesians was intended to strengthen the Church and to make Christians more conscious of their unity in Christ.

Author
The apostle Paul. Paul wrote this letter while he was in prison in Rome. During his first imprisonment Paul wrote what have become known as the "prison letters": Ephesians, Philippians, Colossians and Philemon.

Date
Approximately AD 61–62 while Paul was still in a Roman prison.

Brief outline

1. Introduction *1:1-2*

2. Blessing of the Christian inheritance *1:3–2:22*

3. Paul's work and prayer *3:1-21*

4. The nature of the church *4:1-32*

5. Following Jesus *5:1-20*

6. Living with others *5:21–6:9*

7. Defeating the enemy *6:10-24*

49

Keys to Ephesians
Key thought Christians are to be aware of their position in Christ and draw on his spiritual resources in order to live "a life worthy of the calling you have received" *(4:1)*.

- The phrase "in Christ," or its equivalent, comes more frequently in this letter than any other New Testament book: 35 times.

Philippians
A letter of joy

"Your attitude should be the same as that of Christ Jesus."
Philippians 2:5

Major theme
Christians should not allow their lives to be shaped by outward circumstances but live out the life of Jesus in them. They should experience joy in the Lord, regardless of circumstances, opposition or persecution.

Background and purpose
Paul had been used by God to found the church at Philippi *(Acts 16:11-40)*, and his special love for that church is evident in this letter. They were more sensitive and responsive to his financial needs than any other church *(4:15-18)*. Paul tells them the latest news about his imprisonment *(1:12-20)*. He also takes the opportunity in chapter 3 to warn them about the legalists (Judaizers) and the antinomians (against all laws) who wanted to throw all restraints overboard.

Author
The apostle Paul. He writes this "thank you" letter from his imprisonment in Rome to his Christians friends at Philippi for the gift they had sent him.

Date
When Paul wrote this letter he was expecting imminent execution *(2:17)*. Paul was in fact released from prison shortly after writing this letter in about AD 62.

Brief outline
1. Joy in suffering *1:1-30*
2. Joy in serving Jesus *2:1-30*
3. Joy in Jesus himself *3:1-21*
4. Joy derived from contentment *4:1-23*

50

Key to Philippians
Key words Joy and rejoice.
- 2:5-11 is one of the most crucial passages about Jesus in all of Paul's writings. It contains profound insights in Jesus' pre-existence, incarnation, humiliation and exaltation.

Colossians
Jesus is pre-eminent

"For in Christ all the fullness of the Deity lives in bodily form, and you have been given fullness in Christ, who is the Head over every power and authority."
Colossians 2:9-10

Major theme
Paul writes to oppose a strange teaching that stressed the necessity of fasting, observing special "holy" days and worshiping angels.

Background and purpose
Paul wrote this letter because he heard that heresy was being taught in this church and he felt he had to correct it. One can only deduce the exact nature of the heresy from the way Paul refuted it in *(2:8-23)*. This false teaching held unchristian views on:
• Asceticism *(2:21)*.
• Angel worship *(2:18)*.
• Human wisdom and tradition *(2:4,8)*.
• Secret knowledge, which the Gnostics boasted about *(2:2-3,18)*.

Author
The apostle Paul. Paul was writing to a group of Christians he had never met. The Christian church at Colossae had been founded by Epaphras *(1:4-8; 2:1)*. Paul's large pastoral heart caused him to send this warning letter to "all who had not met me personally" *(2:1)*.

Date
Colossians is one of Paul's "prison letters" and was written from his prison in Rome in approximately AD 61–62.

Brief outline

1. Focus on doctrine – Jesus' deity and pre-eminence *1:1-24*

2. Focus on refuting arguments – the danger of being led astray by false teachers *2:1-23*

3. Focus on conduct – how Christian employers, employees and families should live *3:1-25*

4. Focus on prayer – so that Christians can give a reason for their Christian beliefs *4:1-18*

Keys to Colossians
Key word Fullness.
Key phrase With Christ.
Colossians is perhaps the most Christ-centered book in the Bible.

51

1 Thessalonians
A letter to young Christians

"May the Lord make your love increase and overflow for each other and for everyone else, just as ours does for you. May he strengthen your hearts so that you will be blameless and holy in the presence of our God and Father when our Lord Jesus comes with all his holy ones."
1 Thessalonians 3:12-13

Major theme
1 Thessalonians is a simple follow-up letter to new converts. One major concern is the return of Christ.

Background and purpose
Paul and Silas founded the Christian church in the city of Thessalonica, the capital of Macedonia on Paul's second missionary journey. Paul is anxious to learn how these new Christians are progressing in their Christian lives. The apostle spares them complex doctrine and writes to encourage them. He speaks of the second coming of Jesus as:

• An inspiration for new Christians *(1:10)*.
• A stimulus for Christians to serve God *(2:19)*.
• A comfort for bereaved Christians *(4:18)*.
• An incentive for holy living *(5:23)*.

Author
Paul acknowledges himself as the author of 1 Thessalonians.

Date
Paul wrote this letter from Corinth shortly after leaving Thessalonica around AD 50, making it one of Paul's earliest letters.

Brief outline

1. Greetings and exhortations *1:1–2:20*

2. Paul rejoices over Timothy's report *3:1-13*

3. Exhortation to Christian conduct *4:1-12*

4. Teaching about Jesus' second coming *4:13–5:11*

5. Closing exhortations *5:12-28*

Keys to 1 Thessalonians
Key word Sanctified.
Key teaching God is at work in the life of those who have come to believe.
• The call of God *(1:4; 2:12; 4:7)*.
• The word of God *(1:6,8; 2:13); (4:15)*.
• The will of God *(4:3; 5:18)*.
• The peace of God *(5:23)*.
• The faithfulness of God *(5:24)*.
• Paul describes himself, in his ministry, as being a nurse *(2:7)*, a laborer *(2:9)*, and a father *(2:11)*.

2 Thessalonians
Jesus' second coming

"Concerning the coming of our Lord Jesus Christ and our being gathered to him, we ask you, brothers, not to become easily unsettled or alarmed by some prophecy, report or letter supposed to come from us, saying that the day of the Lord has already come."
2 Thessalonians 2:1-2

Major theme
False teachers were the plague of Paul's life. They had made inroads at Thessalonica. Some went so far as to say that the Day of the Lord had already happened.

Background and purpose
In this letter, Paul writes to encourage the Christians at Thessalonica to withstand persecution and not to give up earning a living. He also corrects some false notions they entertained about Jesus' return.

Paul dictated this letter wanting to make quite sure that any other letter purporting to be from him would not deceive anyone. So he ends by writing: "I, Paul, write this greeting in my own hand, which is the distinguishing mark in all my letters. This is how I write" *(3:18)*.

Author
The apostle Paul wrote his second letter to the Thessalonians from Corinth, probably within six months of his first letter to them, after Silas and Timothy had returned from delivering his first letter to them.

Date
Approximately AD 51.

Brief outline
1. Paul congratulates the Thessalonians on making progress in the Christian life and urges them to endure persecution *1:1-12*

2. Paul corrects false teaching about the day of the Lord *2:1-17*

3. Incorrect behavior caused by wrong beliefs about Jesus' return must be corrected *3:1-18*

Keys to 2 Thessalonians
- 1 and 2 Thessalonians, with Matthew 24–25 and the book of Revelation, are the major sections about prophecy in the New Testament.
- Jesus' return, mentioned 318 times in the New Testament, is the major theme of this letter.
- Paul teaches these new Christians that God is with them. See *1:5,11; 2:13,14; 3:3,16.*

1 Timothy
Advice to ministers

"But you, man of God, flee from all this, and pursue righteousness, godliness, faith, love, endurance and gentleness. Fight the good fight of the faith. Take hold of eternal life to which you were called when you made your good confession in the presence of many witnesses."
1 Timothy 6:11-12

Major theme
Paul, the elderly and experienced apostle, writes to the young timid pastor, Timothy, who faces the great responsibility of caring for the Christians at Ephesus.

Background and purpose
During his fourth missionary journey Paul had "urged" Timothy to "stay there in Ephesus so that" he might "command certain men not to teach false doctrines any longer" *(1:3)*. Paul feared that he might be "delayed" in visiting Timothy and so wrote "these instructions" *(3:14-15)* to help him silence false teachers *(1:3-7; 4:1-8; 6:3-5, 20-21)*, and to organize church worship and the appointment of the right sort of church leaders *(3:1-13; 5:17-25)*.

Author
The apostle Paul. Paul was released from his house arrest in Rome, which is described at the end of the book of Acts, in approx. AD 62–63. He then continued his missionary endeavors for two years or so before being arrested again in approximately AD 64–65, and executed in approximately AD 65–67.

Date
Sometime between Paul's two imprisonments he wrote 1 Timothy and Titus. 1 Timothy was written probably in AD 63–64.

Brief outline

1. Correct teaching *1:1-20*	
2. Public worship *2:1–3:16*	
3. False teaching *4:1-16*	
4. Church discipline *5:1-25*	
5. A pastor's motives *6:1-21*	

Keys to 1 Timothy
- The three letters, 1 and 2 Timothy and Titus, were first referred to as the "Pastoral Epistles" in the 18th century. This is an appropriate name as they focus on the oversight of church life.
- The phrase "God my Savior" is found only in the Pastoral letters *(1 Timothy 1:1; 2:3; 4:10; Titus 1:3; 2:10, 13; 3:4)*.
- 1 Timothy is now regarded as a manual for church leaders.

54

2 Timothy
Paul's last will and testament

"Do your best to present yourself to God as one approved, a workman who does not need to be ashamed and who correctly handles the word of truth."
2 Timothy 2:15

Major theme
Paul's final instructions to his young friend and co-worker, Timothy, is the focus for this book. Paul's unwavering faith and his love for Timothy permeate this letter.

Background and purpose
Paul is facing martyrdom. This letter is made up mostly of personal advice to Timothy. Timothy is told to endure and continue as a faithful witness to Jesus and to keep a good grip on the teaching of the Gospel and of the Old Testament. He is to work as a teacher and an evangelist despite all opposition.

Author
The apostle Paul. When Paul writes his letter he is on his own *(4:10-12)*, awaiting execution, but his case has been postponed *(4:16-17)*.

Date
Paul was arrested and imprisoned under Emperor Nero in AD 65–66. From his cold prison cell Paul wrote this his last letter, AD 66–67.

Brief outline

1. Advice from a father to a son *1:1-18*

2. Advice for all Christian workers *2:1-26*

3. A look at the last days *3:1-17*

4. Paul's last words *4:1-22*

Keys to 2 Timothy
Key word Endure.
Although Paul is facing execution he is very interested in other people. There are 23 references to individuals in this letter.

• Timothy is especially warned to keep clear of "godless chatter" which spreads "like gangrene" *(2:16-17)*.

Titus
How to live as a Christian

"But when the kindness and love of God our Savior appeared, he saved us, not because of righteous things we have done, but because of his mercy. He saved us through the washing of rebirth and renewal by the Holy Spirit ..."
Titus 3:4-5

Major theme
The young pastor, Titus, has been left by Paul to organize the new Christians and the local churches on the island of Crete. Paul's letter is full of practical wisdom on church organization and administration.

Background and purpose
This letter was probably written at the same time and from the same place as 1 Timothy. Titus became a follower of Jesus through Paul, so Paul starts this letter: "To Titus, my true son in our common faith" *(1:4)*. Paul had left Titus in Crete to "straighten out what was left unfinished and appoint elders in every town" *(1:5)*. Paul's letter is crammed with practical advice and warnings about how to deal with false teachers.

Author
The apostle Paul. Paul must have found out that Zenas and Apollos were about to travel through Crete *(3:13)*, thus he took this opportunity of sending a letter by them to Titus.

Date
This letter was written after Paul's first imprisonment in Rome in AD 63–64.

Brief outline

1. Appointment of elders *1:1-16*

2. Advice for different groups of people: older men, older women, young men, young women and servants *2:1-15*

3. Keep going with good deeds, not profitless arguments *3:1-15*

Keys to Titus
Key word Renewal.
Titus 2:11-14 and 3:4-7 are two of the most comprehensive statements about the Gospel in the New Testament.
- 2:13 refutes the accusation that Paul forgot about Jesus' return towards the end of his life.

Philemon
Take back your runaway slave

"Perhaps the reason he was separated from you for a little while was that you might have him back for good – no longer as a slave, but better than a slave, as a dear brother." *Philemon 15-16*

Major theme
Paul's shortest letter is a model of tact and concern for the forgiveness of one who might otherwise face harsh punishment, if not death.

Background and purpose
When Tychicus arrived in Colossae he came with a letter to the Christians there, as well as with this letter to Philemon, who lived in Colossae. Tychicus also brought Onesimus with him. "Tychicus will tell you all the news about me. ... He is coming with Onesimus, our faithful and dear brother, who is one of you." *Colossians 4:7, 9*

Onesimus was a runaway slave. He found Paul in prison and became a Christian, probably with the help of Paul, as Paul calls him "my son Onesimus" in v.10. Now Paul is sending Onesimus back to his owner, Philemon. Paul hopes that this letter will enable Philemon to receive Onesimus back, "no longer as a slave, but better than a slave, as a dear brother" (*16*).

Author
The apostle Paul. Paul was in prison, most probably in Rome, when he wrote this letter.

Date
Approximately AD 61.

Brief outline

1. Paul gives thanks for Philemon *1-7*

2. Pleads for his runaway slave Onesimus *8-16*

3. Paul reminds Philemon that he owes his own Christian life to him *17-25*

57

Keys to Philemon
Key word Welcome.

Hebrews
Good news about better things

"Therefore, since we are surrounded by such a great cloud of witnesses, let us throw off everything that hinders and the sin that so easily entangles, and let us run with perseverance the race marked out for us." *Hebrews 12:1*

Major theme
The basic theme of Hebrews is found in the use of the word "better/superior" *(1:4; 6:9; 7:7, 19, 22; 8:6; 9:23; 10:34; 11:16, 35, 40; 12:24)*. Jesus is shown to be superior to Judaism.

Background and purpose
The book was addressed to Jewish Christians who were facing persecution and were being tempted to compromise their faith and return to the practices of Judaism. The author warns them against regarding Christianity as merely an offshoot of Judaism and encourages them to persevere in their faith.

Author
The authorship of Hebrews remains a mystery inasmuch as no direct identification is possible within the book. Traditionally, Paul has been credited as the author. Other suggested authors are Luke, Barnabas and Apollos.

Date
Because the fall of Jerusalem and the ending of the Old Testament sacrificial system is not mentioned in this letter it is assumed that it was written before AD 70. If the persecution mentioned *(chapter 10)* was caused by Nero, then this letter must be dated after the fire of Rome, approximately AD 64.

Brief outline

1. The superiority of the Son over the prophets and angels *1:1–2:18*

2. The superiority of the Son over Moses and Joshua *3:1–4:16*

3. The superiority of Jesus' priesthood over the Jewish priesthood *5:1–8:5*

4. The superiority of the new covenant over the old covenant *8:6–10:39*

5. The importance of faith *11:1–13:25*

Keys to Hebrews
Key words Heaven/heavenly, used 18 times, to show that Christianity is spiritual. Once/once for all, used nine times, to show the finality of God's revelation in Jesus.
Key chapter Chapter 11, the Bible's hall of fame of those who lived by faith in God in Old Testament times, even if it meant suffering or martyrdom.
• Jesus is depicted as our eternal High Priest according to the order of Melchizedek. *7:1-28*

James
Practical Christianity

"As the body without the spirit is dead, so faith without deeds is dead." *James 2:26*

Major theme

James writes as a pastor, rebuking and encouraging Christians. He stresses the importance of putting faith into practical action.

Background and purpose

James is full of practical advice about Christian conduct.
• For Christians under pressure *(see 1:2-4)*
• For wealthy Christians *(see 1:9-11, 5:1-6)*
• As church members *(see 2:1-9)*
The letter emphasizes practical Christianity and often echoes Jesus' teaching in the Sermon on the Mount *(Matthew 5–7)*.

Author

James, the half-brother of Jesus. During Jesus' lifetime this James was not a believer *(John 7:2-5)*, but he saw Jesus after the resurrection *(1 Corinthians 15:7)*, and was present on the day of Pentecost *(Acts 1:14)*. He became leader of the church in Jerusalem *(Acts 12:17; 15:13)*. He was martyred about AD 62.

Date

Before AD 62. Because of its strong Jewish feel, a date of AD 48–49 or even earlier is often suggested for its writing. This date would make it one of the earliest New Testament letters.

Brief outline

1. Living faith is tested by trial *1:1-27*

2. Living faith is proved by deeds *2:1-26*

3. Living faith is revealed in behavior *3:1–4:17*

4. Living faith is exercised by persecution *5:1-20*

Keys to James

• James describes God as the One who comes close to us *(4:6-8)*, a perfect description of Jesus.
• James has been called the "Proverbs of the New Testament" because it is similar in style and content to the wisdom books of the Old Testament, especially Proverbs.
• James has also been called the "Amos of the New Testament" because of his hard-hitting teaching against social injustice.
• James differs from all other New Testament letters in that:
• It only mentions Jesus twice, *1:1, 2:1*.
• It is the most Jewish book in the New Testament with many Old Testament references.
• It has many allusions to the Sermon on the Mount *(1:2,4,5,20,22; 2:10,13; 3:18; 4:4,10,11,12; 5:2,3,10,12)*, and other teachings of Jesus.
• It is packed full of punchy proverbs.

1 Peter
A message for suffering Christians

"Dear friends, do not be surprised at the painful trial you are suffering, as though something strange were happening to you. But rejoice that you participate in the sufferings of Christ, so that you may be overjoyed when his glory is revealed."
1 Peter 4:12-13

Major theme
Peter wrote this letter to encourage those Christians who were downhearted because of the persecution they were suffering.

Background and purpose
Peter gives his readers practical advice about how to react as they endure undeserved suffering. They are to stand firm. Peter bases his teaching on the example set by Jesus towards such suffering. Peter wanted to overcome any attitude of bitterness and anxiety with an attitude of dependence on and confidence in God. Peter's words are to remind Christians of their conversion, the privileges they have in Christ, and the holy lives they are to live.

Author
Peter the apostle. Peter wrote from "Babylon" *(5:13)*, a code name for Rome.

Date
This letter was written in AD 63–64 as the most vicious persecutions under Emperor Nero were gathering steam, shortly before Peter himself suffered martyrdom under that regime.

Brief outline

1. Christian salvation *1:1–2:10*

2. Christian relationships, in pagan society, political life, at work, in the family and when treated unfairly *2:11–3:12*

3. Christian suffering *3:13–4:19*

4. Christians in the community *5:1-14*

Keys to 1 Peter
Key word Suffer, used 15 times.
Key phrase Strangers in the world.
- Peter writes as one who is always thinking about his days as Jesus' disciple.
- Peter recalls the death of Jesus *(2:22-25)*.
- Peter appears to be reflecting on his encounter with Jesus after the resurrection (5:2, *see John 21:15-23*).

60

2 Peter
No passive journey

"For prophecy never had its origin in the will of man, but men spoke from God as they were carried along by the Holy Spirit."
2 Peter 1:21

Major theme
The need for growth in the grace and knowledge of Jesus. The need to stay diligent.

Background and purpose
This letter has been called Peter's "swan song", as he left this letter to guide those who would carry on after his death:

"I think it right to refresh your memory as long as I live in the tent of this body, because I know that I will soon put it aside ..." *(1:13-14)*.

Peter writes to help with three great problems facing his readers:

• the temptation to become complacent and sit back;
• vicious false teaching from people who were "like brute beasts, creatures of instinct" *(2:12)*
• cynicism about the delay in Jesus' return.

Author
The apostle Peter. The writer of this letter calls himself "Simon Peter" in the opening verse and claims to have been an eyewitness to the transfiguration of Jesus, which we know was only seen by Peter, Andrew and John. "We were eyewitnesses of his majesty. ... We ourselves heard this voice that came from heaven when we were with him on the sacred mountain." *(1:16,18)*

Date
Peter wrote this letter after he wrote 1 Peter, "this is now my second letter to you" *(3:1)*, and before AD 68, as he was martyred in Nero's reign of terror. It was written shortly before Peter's death, "I know that I will soon put it [the tent of this body] aside, as our Lord Jesus Christ has made clear to me" *(1:14)*, in AD 65–66.

Brief outline

1. Cultivate a Christian character *1:1-21*

2. False teachers are condemned *2:1-22*

3. Have confidence that Jesus will return *3:1-18*

Keys to 2 Peter
Key word Knowledge (of God), used 16 times, in its various forms.
Key thought The best antidote to false teaching is correct understanding of the truth.

1, 2, & 3 John
Knowing and being sure

"I write these things to you who believe in the name of the Son of God so that you may know that you have eternal life." *1 John 5:13*
"And this is love: that we walk in obedience to his commands. As you have heard from the beginning, his command is that you walk in love." *2 John 6*
"I have no greater joy than to hear that my children are walking in the truth." *3 John 4*

Major theme
- **1 John**'s theme is assurance; the tests for discovering false teaching.
- **2 John** has a warning against denying the incarnation and emphasizes the necessity of obeying God's command of love.
- **3 John** is about how to be witnesses to the truth.

Background and purpose
The elderly John wrote these fatherly letters out of loving concern for his "children," whose steadfastness in the truth was being threatened by the lure of worldliness and the guile of false teachers.

Author
The apostle John. None of these letters name an author, but their style and range of ideas indicate a single author. The author claims to have been an eyewitness of Jesus' life *(1 John 1:1-3)*. The letters have many words and thought forms which are the same as John's Gospel. Compare John 5:24 with 1 John 3:14 and John 1:14,18; 3:16 with 1 John 4:9.

Date
It is not possible to place the writings of these three letters to a precise year, but it is most probable that they were written towards the end of John's life, around AD 85–95.

Brief outline
1 John

1. The basis of fellowship
1:1–2:27

2. The characteristics of fellowship *2:28–5:3*

3. The consequences of fellowship *5:4-21*

2 John

1. Abide in God's commandments *1-6*

2. Avoid false teachers *7-13*

3 John

1. Gaius' commendation *1-8*

2. Diotrephes' condemnation *9-14*

Keys to 1, 2, & 3 John
Key words Fellowship, in 1 John; love, in 2 John; and truth, in 3 John.

Jude
Coping with heresy

"Dear friends, although I was very eager to write to you about the salvation we share, I felt I had to write and urge you to contend for the faith that was once for all entrusted to the saints."
Jude verse 3

Major theme
Jude had intended to write a letter about salvation *(3)*, but because of the threats against his readers he turns his attention instead to those who were seeking to destroy the gospel.

Background and purpose
Jude warned his readers against the evil people who were trying to use the gospel for their own ends. Jude told them that it was important that they defended the gospel. Jude ends his letter with a series of practical exhortations aimed to strengthen their Christian lives.

Author
Jude. Jude identifies himself as "a brother of James" *(1)*. This would make Jude a brother, or, to be more accurate, half-brother of Jesus. He was clearly a humble man as he also calls himself a "servant of Jesus Christ" in the opening verse.

Date
If Peter made use of Jude in his second letter, as seems probable, then Jude must be dated before 2 Peter, that is AD 64–65.

Brief outline

1. Jude's concern about the influence of false teachers *1-4*

2. Jude's description of the false teachers *5-16*

3. Jude's defense against false teachers *17-23*

4. Jude's powerful doxology *24-25*

Keys to Jude
• **Key word** Keep.
• Jude quotes two books that are not in the Bible.
The Book of Enoch, see 14-15, was a popular religious book in those days.
The Assumption of Moses, see verse 9.
Jude does not quote these books as if they had equal authority as books of the Bible, but as a preacher today might use a quotation from Shakespeare to illustrate what he was saying.

Revelation
A glimpse into the future

"'Write, therefore, what you have seen, what is now and what will take place later.'"
Revelation 1:19

Major theme
The book of Revelation is called an "apocalyptic" book as it unveils and reveals truth in a vivid and poetic way. It is an encouragement to withstand persecution and centers round Jesus who alone has authority to judge the earth and to rule it in righteousness.

Background and purpose
There are four main approaches to interpreting this book.

• **The preterist view** focuses on the events that happened when the book was written, which would have all been known by the first readers. There is no need to look for any detailed revelation in this book about our own times.

• **The historic view** sees Revelation as one long outline of history, from the first century to today.

• **The futurist view** ignores all possible historical allusions and teaches that the book refers only to the end times.

• **The symbolic view** sees symbols in every passage. They can be interpreted without any reference to world history.

Perhaps the best way to interpret the book of Revelation is to combine these four approaches. Then, for example, the prophecies in the book can be taken as referring to the time of dreadful persecution under Domitian in the first century *and* to events of the end time.

Author
The apostle John. The author is named as "John" four times *(1:1,4,9; 22:8)*.

Date
The first major persecution took place under Nero and seems to be reflected in Revelation. The second, even fiercer persecution, under Emperor Domitian, lasted from AD 91–95 which is the most likely time for the writing of Revelation.

Brief outline

1. **Chapter 1:** "What you have seen" *(1:19)*

2. **Chapter 2–3** "What is now" *(1:19)*

3. **Chapters 4–22:** "What will take place later" *(1:19)*
• John's view of heaven *4:1–5:14*
• Times of tribulation *6:1–19:21*
• The thousand years and final judgment *20:1-15*
• The new heaven and new earth *21:1–22:21*